TRANSYLVANIA
Sibenburgen.

Milliaria Germanica communis

Amsterdami, Apud Guiljelmum et Ioannem Blaeu.

Hans Berg

Siebenbürgen

A Picture Book of Transylvania

Photographic Credits to: Erhart Daniel, Annemarie Schiel, Hermann Buresch, Hans Baumhartner, Josef Fischer, Karl Lehmann

Published in English by: The Alliance of Transylvanian Saxons, Cleveland, Ohio, U.S.A.

Printed and Bound by: Wort und Welt Verlag, Innsbruck, Austria

4

Transylvania,
one of the most Restless Landscapes in Europe

Transylvania, host of nations!
With the climate of all regions,
And the garland of various peoples,
Gathered 'round the homeland's altar.

(The fourth verse of the Transylvanian-
Saxons' national song; lyrics by Max Molt-
ke, music by Johann Lukas Hedwig)

Frontispiece:
Statue of St. Catherine in the Black
Church of Kronstadt

Page 2 and 3:
Ruins of the Cistercian Abbey of Kerz

Left:
Portcullis in the Church of Wurmloch

Following double page:
A flock of sheep with the Southern
Carpathians in the background

To this day it is one of the most restless landscapes in Europe. The continual coming and going, appearance and disappearance of peoples, which started long before Christ, blows through it like the breath of almighty time, determines the heartbeat of its epochs and seems to be its cardinal and inexorable law.

If Ferdinand Gregorovius, the brilliant portrayer of medieval Rome and unforgettable tracer of geopsychological forces, had known it, he would not have hesitated for a moment to classify it as 'The magnetism of history,' something which he felt was very much active in Europe's great historical landscapes. Over and above the conceivable beauty of mountains and rivers, the riches gathered from the fields and the soil and from the gold- and silver-bearing veins, these landscapes exert an inexplicable fascination. Often the attraction does not have anything to do with material aspects. The aura left on them by time continues to vibrate undisturbed for hundreds, even thousands of years. They touch everybody who enters them with the breath of the living, and with every step transfer one back to former ages, as if one were suspended in time and suddenly one understands why this or that event, tragedy, triumph and decay had to happen here and in this very way. A force runs through them which binds history together and extinguishes all concept of time – a force which turns yesterday into today and today into yesterday. Anyone who has ever crossed the Apulian Murge in the glowing summer of the south, following the traces left by the Hohenstaufens, anyone who has rambled through the world of Spanish-Arab castles and towns on the high plateau of the shimmering Castilian la Manche, who, in the warm light of the Provence, has wandered along Roman military roads and passed columns of Jupiter and Franconian fortresses, anyone who has roamed about the Peloponnese in the burning wind from Tirins to Mykene, will have also felt this force. And one feels it again, when one enters the forests and mountains of the highlands between the Southern and Eastern Carpathians and Transylvania.

When the cavalry generals of the sons of Genghis Khan (the blue-eyed, blond-haired Mongol emperor who founded an empire, unrivaled in history, on the blood of the most cultured peoples of Asia) invaded Europe by the ancient trade-route running west of the Caspian Sea and north of the Black Sea, they, the best army captains of the century, sent the strong southern flank of the Golden Horde to the Transylvanian Highlands. Their strategic tactics were: if one wants to conquer Europe from the east, one must close the pincer of the armies over the Carpathian arc.

The Mongols were advancing, in fact, on a route which another Asian tribe of horsemen, the Huns, had taken nine hundred years earlier. Only after they had reached the Carpathian Highlands had the Huns felt secure enough to proceed into South-East Europe and break through to the West and the mediterranean South – right up to the river banks of the Loire and the gates of Rome.

More than five hundred years after the Huns the Magyar horsemen – the terror of Europe – took the same road into the Highlands and, once in the Pannonian Plain, began devastating raids on Bavaria,

Sentry walk in the fortified church of Hamruden

Thuringia, Swabia and Northern Italy, until they were forced back by Otto the Great.

In the middle of the 20th century, one and a half millenia after the Huns, approximately one thousand years after the Magyars and almost exactly seven hundred years after the legendary cavalry divisions of Khagan Ogadai had swept over the Highlands, the Soviet marshals set their strongest troops on this route in their last assault on the retreating German armies. During the fights for control of these passes in 1944 more people died than during the defense and fall of Stalingrad.

The strategic principle of taking possession of the Carpathians from the east and southeast had, however, been operated very much earlier, namely by the commanders of the legions of the Imperium Romanum. The Highlands of the Carpathian Basin, they used to say, were the 'First protruding into the heart of Germany,' by which they meant the center of the Continent, which, at that time, was covered by the settlements of the restless and unpredictable Germanic tribes. One of these tribes – the Bastarnae – gave its name to that area of the Carpathians which begins northeast of Vienna and stretches in a wide arc right over to the Danube delta and which used to be called the Alpes Bastarnicae . . .

It is, indeed, remarkable that during those centuries on record not only was the east-southeast movement time and again magnetically attracted by this region but, likewise, the movement from the opposite direction. The first Germano-Roman clashes were by no means the earliest to take place here, for even before that – about one hundred years B.C. – the Teutons stood here face to face with Gaius Marius at Aquae Sextiae and the Cimbri tribe at Campi Raudii. In fact, one could start with the imperious, self-confident Bastarnae, who used to inhabit the Carpathian Highlands as early as 500 B.C. and who, sometimes alone and sometimes as the allies of Mithradates and the Getae, attacked the frontiers of the Roman Empire. They were the first of a number of fierce Germanic tribes who invaded these Highlands from the north – with a dynamic force that was equally feared and admired throughout European history.

The impetuous Vandals – they came from Silesia, which was named after one of their tribes, the Silingi – settled here before their march to Spain and into North Africa, as far as Carthage. The Visigoths, one of the most ardent and cultured Germanic tribes, founded an empire in this region, enclosed like a huge cirque by the mountain ranges, and forced Rome to conclude a treaty of withdrawal. Their famous bishop, Ulfilas, led the Arian Christians from here to the south and today a village in western Transylvania still bears their name: Gotatea. The Langobardi were at home in this region and left their mark on architecture and tomb sculpture before they broke into Byzantine Italy. Ostrogoths maintained their rulers' residence near today's Apahida in northern Transylvania before they migrated to the Pannonic Basin. Four hundred years after Christ the East-Germanic Gepidae, who hailed from the Vistula, founded an empire in the Carpathian Highlands and their princes' tombs, found near Klausenburg, with the wonderful pectoral made from gold and almandine bears witness to the culture and strength of a people who defeated Attila's sons but a hundred years later themselves were hewn to pieces by the allied Langobardi and Asian Avars in a murderous battle at the river Mieresch, which flows right through the middle of Transylvania. Notwithstanding, there is proof that as late as the end of the 12th century the Gepidae still lived in Transylvania.

Since time immemorial the many-faceted and at the same time uniform region of South-East Europe, encircled by the Black, the Aegean, Ionian and Adriatic Sea, has been the most important transit area as well as the bridge between Europe and Asia, between Asia and Europe. Even by just glancing at the map the eye is struck by its geographical uniformity – a *terra uniforma* stretching from Trieste to the mouth of the Dniester, from the Peloponnese to Transylvania and covering an area of about 270,000 square miles.

The Carpathian Highlands have always – but in the past more so than today – occupied a key position in this area. They lie exactly on the way of the new-comer from the east, on the oldest and climate-wise most favourable route leading from the settled regions of Asia to Europe – as an extension of the Chinese silk route and at about the same latitude that runs through Mongolia. At the same time, however, the Carpathian arc, starting on the fringe of Central Europe and covering about 900 miles, served as the natural railguard for the migration from the opposite direction, the northwest, thus bringing to this region various Germanic peoples, tribes and groups too. Following the law of migration from different directions, of peoples not just arriving in this region but, in particular, encountering others here, this landscape was bound to become a meeting place of historical significance, the hub of potent forces.

For some strange reason none of the peoples which this landscape absorbed in the centuries after Attila – Avars, Magyars, Pechenegs and Kumans from the Asian East, Celts, Slavs from the neighbouring region – survived here for very long, as was exactly the case with the Germans who pushed down from the north, or the Dacians after whom, for centuries, this region was named or the Romans and various Asian tribes. And every time the explosive effect, brought about by the clashes between these peoples thinking in Continental dimensions and touching each other like fire and water, had something of the inevitable and final about it.

For as much as they fought one another in the centuries of the continuous and heinous war which we call the migration of peoples, not one of them was able to hold its ground. All these intelligent and vital, savage and fearless peoples and tribes, blown relentlessly by history from all directions of the wind, into the spell of the Carpathian arc – all of them were hurled out of the vulcano funnel of this landscape, died out, were crushed and wiped out by stronger tribes, were absorbed into the stream of new arrivals or broke away to other regions.

German peasant woman from Transylvania – 'Love and sorrow, time and eternity . . .'

Transylvanian-Saxon linen embroidery: pillow-case, Mühlbach

'The peaks of the Carpathians . . .'

With the Belt of the Karpaten round the Growing Dress of Crop-green

Transylvania, land of blessings,
Land of fullness and of pow'r!
With the belt of the Karpaten
Round the growing dress of crop-green,
Land of gold, of grape and wine.

(The first verse of the Transylvanian-
Saxons' national song)

Sometimes the mountains seem to encircle the Highlands like phantastic paintings.

There are late summer evenings full of heavy light and barely describable melancholy, when they appear scattered all around the dark countryside like the smoldering logs of a giant fire quivering with gold and copper. But in the harsh midday light of the southern sun rays the peasants see them from their fields as lightblue glass plates, as if broken in anger and leant against the sky by a human hand and forgotten there. In clear weather they can be seen from every undulation of the innermost parts of the country. During the icy winters dry desert cold is carried by the Ukrainian winds through their eastern passes between the Golden Bistritz and the Vrancea Mountains; a cold which makes the blood curdle. That is when they appear to be truly the lords of the Highlands, glistening visibly on the frontiers of these foothills. In August the scorching heat waves from the Danube lowlands roll northwards with the same lack of restraint, across the gorges and glacial valleys of the Southern Carpathian range rendering the inhabitants breathless and turning Transylvania, from Kronstadt in the south to Klausenburg in the north, into a shimmering den of heat.

The artists among the peoples living there have tried to capture all their moods, their ever-changing faces. They have not only depicted the play of colors at different times of the day and the year but have at the same time tried to put on canvas the smell of the endless beech and fir-tree forests, of the mountain pastures, the archaic and undisturbed river scenes.

The massifs of the Eastern and Southern Carpathians, describing an arc of about five hundred miles, together with the Transylvanian Ore Mountains in the west belong to one of the most undisturbed and varied mountainous regions in Europe.

They encircle rolling highlands of an average elevation of 1,800 feet above sea level and an area of well over 23,000 square miles, i. e. about half the area but with four million inhabitants just one third of the population of Pennsylvania. The northernmost town – Bistritz – is at about the latitude of Seattle and the southernmost town – Kronstadt – is at the latitude of Portland, Oregon. Between the Pietrosul Peak in the far northeast (on the upper fringe of the beginning of the arc), the Omul Peak near the bend of the arc and the Peleaga Peak at its southwestern end there is an uninterrupted series of mountain ranges cut only by river valleys and pass roads – the geological structure of these ranges corresponds to that of the Alps. Their highest peaks reach 7,620 feet. Their area is much greater than that of the highlands bounded by them.

There is nothing in the Highlands which could not be derived from these mountains. They are the storehouse of immense natural resources. They offer a panorama of endless beauty. They are the mythical power and center of a landscape which belongs solely to them – regardless of all its past, present and future inhabitants.

The courses of their rivers and brooks, such as the Golden Bistritz, which crosses the Eastern- and the river Alt, which breaks through the Southern Carpathians, cut themselves deep into the lime-

Fogarasch Mountains in the Southern Carpathians

Following double page:
Carpathian winter landscape near Kronstadt, oil canvas by Heinrich Schunn

16

stone layers of the mountain ranges as well as into the quartz veins of the deeply embedded rock. Here one finds the earliest proven gold in Europe – that is, the alluvial gold of the rivers and the native gold of the mountains. There is evidence that gold-mining in Transylvania dates at least as far back as those times when the Egyptians were washing their gold nuggets in the Blue Nile – that is 2000 B.C., in the era of the middle Helladic culture in the Aegean Sea. Roman, Lydian and Phoenician gold extraction is of more recent origin. As late as in the Middle and Late Middle Ages most of the gold in Europe was obtained from the mines and rivers of the Carpathians.

Not only gold, however, but also the rich salt stock, stretching from the mountains across the Highlands, attracted the peoples – horsemen, herdsmen and farmers – of earliest ages. This salt vein started, here alongside the salt lakes and salines, some of the most legendary and notorious salt routes ever known. Trickery, murder and homicide were used in the fighting and haggling for possession of these routes, no matter whither they led – be it the Hallstattian route in the Salzkammergut or the one at the Franconian Saale. It is no coincidence that Avarian and Alanian horsemen's graves were found principally on the borders of the old salt route or that archeologists came across a Celtic necropolis in the environs of the salines.

Was it any different this century, when we think about the fighting and squabbling over the rich oil-deposits in the sedimentary rock of the South Carpathian slopes? . . .

Deep in these mountains, beneath the layers of sand and clay, there are deposits of natural gas, of carbon, of various ores, of uranium, manganese and copper as well as marble of the highest quality.

Just as salt and bread have gone down as the oldest symbols of Man's requirements and Man's wealth, so water and forests are the most important possessions of the mountains.

About fifty large courses of water run loose from the Eastern and Southern Carpathians. They flow through several countries and then into the Danube. Although their headwaters are very close to one another, they flow in different directions, as through driven away from each other by invisible forces. They force their way through mountain ranges as waterfalls and rapids of unrestrained beauty, develop into dreamlike lakes, shimmer through dusky forests – the Golden Bistritz eastward, the Alt southward, the Mieresch and Kreisch rivers to the west and the Samosch to the north. It is as if in the beautiful scenery of the Highlands the historical magnetism once again strains to play a role. Throughout history, the passages through the ring of the mountains by which the rivers open up the Highlands in all directions, have served as gateways, as thresholds and barrages, for in the course of the millenia dozens of fierce fights and decisive battles took place at all of them. All of these rivers were stained with the blood of innumerable warriors; some of them turned red in the process.

But when the battle was over, the shepherds, with their flocks of sheep, would return to their banks and today the men in the Rodna Mountains still tie together rafts of huge fir trees and go down the

The northern approach to the Red Tower Pass

roaring rapids of the Golden Bistritz towards the rising sun. Likewise today, barefooted girls and woman from high up in the Transylvanian Ore Mountains still rinse their snow-white linen clothes in the water of these rivers; and cattle drivers take their cows, horses and black buffaloes to water at the fords in the plains and basins of the Highlands. They drink the water of these strange rivers, which appear from out of nowhere and then vanish back into the mountains again. With their waywardness these rivers represent the dynamic element of the Carpathian world.

And then, as though to introduce some calm, there are the forests everywhere, those thick Transylvanian forests that have been praised and honored thousands of times both in lively and sad songs. These forests, whose rustling fills the days and nights, represent the tranquil part of the landscape.

Anyone who has ever rambled through the iridiscent darkness of the pine forests in the north, in the Marmarosch, eastward of Borşa, will have felt this calm. Not too long ago here on young, moss-covered forest plantations, used to dwell the bearded and hunchbacked European bison, the image of which has been preserved for over ten thousand years in the caves of Altamira, Lascaux and Addaura. Here, in the northeastern part of the Carpathian forests he became, not surprisingly, the legendary and heraldic animal of early chieftains and founders of tribes.

The virginity of Carpathian woodlands is repeated further south in the Căliman and Hargita Mountains, whose extensive beech and pine forests seem like the very calm breath of Earth itself. In early, bright autumn nights the bellowing of the red deer is heard as far away as down below in the village settlements. In winter, before the break of day, the starving wolves howl behind stables and cowsheds.

This virgin calm is felt even more so in the wooded valleys and gorges of the Southern Carpathians, where from thickly forested, rugged and inaccessible gorges rise the highest peaks of the entire Carpathian arc: the ranges south of the Alt Valley and the Burzenland – the Fogarasch Mountains, the Königstein, the Bucegi-massif. Their majestic beauty inspired a well-known poet to call them 'God's open picture book'.

On the high mountain pastures grows the rust-leaved alpine rose, whose scent on summer nights can be caught even way down in the basin of this mountainous region. Here, on August nights, the chamois drink in herds of a few hundred at the mountain lakes of the Bulea and Podragu cirque. The rock faces resound with their galloping hooves as soon as they are startled by some noise that propels them into one of their daring sprints through the vertical precipices. It can happen that on the ridges of the jagged mountain ranges the leader of a flock of sheep slips and takes the whole herd down with him. That is when the golden eagles appear and with shrill hunting cries they swoop down on to the cadavers and tear them to pieces before the shepherds are able to recover them. In the early mists of the summer mornings the clearings in the oak-woods of the foothills resemble steaming fields stampeded and trampled down by herds of wild boars.

Buffalo herd near Baassen

Right: Caraiman peaks in the Bucegi
massif
Below: Carpathian meadows

26

Above: Cherry-blossom time in Michelsberg

Left: The 'Broken Tower' guarding the approach to the Red Tower Pass

The king of these mountain forests is not, however, the golden eagle, the lynx, the roe deer of the forests of the Bihor Mountains, the wolf, the chamois, the wild boar or the stag of the northern parts but the Carpathian bear.

He is a mixture of easy-going laziness and awesome strength. He can reach a weight of up to 1,300 pounds. With a single blow of his paw he can crush the spine of a full-grown draft ox, as if it were a piece of dry wood the thickness of one's finger. He is capable of dragging a buffalo bait through the undergrowth of the forest more quickly than the hunter is able to follow. At night on the farms of the high pastures of the Rodna Mountains he steals into the sheep pens with the light-footedness of a dancer and, as quick as lightning, strikes down three animals and retreats only at the last minute as the shepherds come running towards him with burning logs; for a long time after the valley resounds with their shouting and the accompanying yelping of the hounds.

The bear has always been at home in the deep forests of the Bucegi foothills, in the mighty valleys around the Hoher Rong – skeletons of his forebear from the Ice Age, the cave bear, were found only some years ago in the grottoes of the Steinmilch Cave in this region.

He is, however, more than just the feared giant amongst the animals in the Carpathians who still dare to come at night right up to the entrance of the villages and towns on the southern fringe of the Burzenland. Just as his cousins in Alaska, Siberia, Greenland, Ceylon or Malaya are to the trappers, fur hunters and foresters of those preserves, so the Carpathian bear has also been to all the peoples of Transylvania the embodiment of an unflinching force, of reasonableness and a gruff easy-going nature, and despite his instinct to prey on others, Man has always had a closer relationship with him than with any other animal. In the fairy-tales, popular poetry, idioms, jokes and literature of all the peoples dwelling here – the Romanians, Germans, Hungarians and the gypsies – the bear has been given the same interpretation, almost as if there was only one bear.

Those who speak of the Carpathian bear also know about the many 'Bear Caves' of Transylvania. Right in the middle of the Southern Carpathians, in the mountains near Mühlbach, there is, for example, the Şura-Mare-Cave, which is more than four miles long and is filled with the thundering sound of fifty waterfalls. In the Transylvanian Ore Mountains, north of the moonlike lake-country of the Retezat Mountains, one finds the Pojarul-Poliţei Stalactite Cavern with the awesome and irregularly shaped sinter formations. Nearby is one of the most impressive karst wonders of the world: the merging and overlapping Cetăţile-Ponorului Cave with subterranean domes, huge caverns, waterfalls and rapids, which can be mastered only by boats. After squeezing themselves through the crevasses of the cross-bedded rock of the East Carpathian Rodna Mountains, spelaeologists discovered the well-like abysses of the Izvorul-Tăuşoarelor group of caves. Close to the upper course of the Schnelle Kreisch, near Suncuiuş, there is the entrance to the famous Wind Cave – eleven miles of caverns, passages, abysses, shafts, slopes, gorges and craters distributed

'Carpathian bear,' charcoal drawing by Fritz Kimm

Following double page: Krähenstein (Ciucas), Southern Carpathians

over five floors. The greatest of the subterranean wonders is, however, the sinister Topolniţa Labyrinth in the western foothills of the Southern Carpathians – it measures more than twelve miles in length.

Since time immemorial this empire of subterranean stone vaults has been spreading beneath every step made by the Transylvanian shepherds and hunters, lumberers and forest-keepers, heyducks and berry collectors...

It comes as no surprise that for Man these mountains and forests have always meant far more than mere material property and resources, such as gold and salt, timber and ore, that in fact, even in this century they have served as a refuge for fleeing people and partisans. For all those who have ever settled here the mountains and forests have, in some way or other represented part of the mythical landscape of Transylvania, which concerned itself neither with their language, nor with their race or religion.

Landscape always means more than just an optical picture. The things going on in it can never be explained merely in relation to their outer appearance. Landscapes are reservoirs of invisible powers and driving forces, which influence historical events at least as much as figures or the logics of political or military strength or social conventions.

'Romanian shepherd boy,' charcoal drawing by Fritz Kimm

Transylvania, the Land of the Fortified Churches

Near Marienburg, near Marienburg,
Where Weiß so bravely fell.
His name is unforgotten,
His resting place unknown.

(The second verse of the song "Near
Marienburg", lyrics by Fr. W. Schuster,
music probably by Johann Hellwig)

Rosenau Castle, Burzenland (area near
Kronstadt)

Above: Approach to the fortified church of Tartlau

Left: The fortified church of Eibesdorf

Above: The fortified church of Tartlau. Emergency quarters in the central court of the fortified structure, in which the villagers found refuge in times of siege.

Right: Törzburg Castle on Dietrichstein Mountain

In April 1612, the garrison at Rosenau Castle, in the extreme southeast of Transylvania, opened their gates after receiving a promise that they would be spared by the Magyar troops, who had besieged them.

The besiegers, about seven thousand horsemen clad in armor and howitzer cannoneers on horseback, let the four hundred men, women and children who had taken refuge in the Castle go unmolested, in fact, they scarcely took any notice of them. A colonel, sword in hand, demanded that the leader of the castle defenders be brought before him dead or alive. Without further ado a seventy year old man with shoulder-length hair stepped out of the frightened crowd, went up to the officer and said, 'My name is Pitter Durmes. What is it that you want of me?' 'Take him to the Prince', roared the colonel to some of the mercenaries standing behind him.

As it later turned out, the seven thousand horsemen despite their dozen howitzers had not stood a chance of capturing the Castle, which was built on a precipitous cone – it was simply that the defenders' morale and economic resources were exhausted after decades of fighting between princes and voivodes for control of the devastated country. The degree of their exhaustion was evident in that the besieged garrison decided to surrender although they knew that the Prince's troops had also promised the defenders of neighbouring Zeiden Castle that they could leave honourably but had then impaled them alive.

Half an hour after the opening of the castle gates Pitter Durmes, elected sheriff of Rosenau and, therefore, in times of war acting commander of the garrison, stood before the very young Prince of Transylvania, Gabriel Báthory, the last scion of a formerly distinguished Hungarian noble family. Nothing has ever been recorded about the encounter between the arrogant young Prince and the sheriff, who up to the last minute had continued to oppose the surrender of the Castle. His release by the Prince, without being executed, Durmes owed solely to his white hair. But what he had previously suspected, now became even more obvious: this time, as the one before, the Prince would break his word.

In fact, Báthory did not for one moment intend to keep his promise and not harm the defenders if they surrendered. What now began to take place exceeded the latter's worst fears.

Showing neither shame nor pity the soldiers ran amok in the village, comprising eighty farms, on which the German Emperor and Hungarian King Sigismund had conferred the market rights in 1427. The men were killed or hanged, whenever they rebelled, the women raped, the wells befouled and filled up, the cattle – that which had not been driven into the nearby mountain forests – slaughtered and all the remaining food pillaged. Lastly, the retreating hordes set fire to the barns and houses. The Castle, where meanwhile the Prince's guards were billeted, had to be ransomed at a high price. In short, no destruction, humiliation or sorrow was spared these people.

A contemporary chronicler tells us that Báthory had, apparently, a particular reason for his excessive and senseless rage.

Preceding double page:
The village of Frauendorf

Right: The choir of the church at Michelsberg Castle

On inspecting the castle walls rising from the rocks, and the powerful towers, the outer defenses, the trapdoors and the cleverly arranged domestic buildings inside the Castle as well as the spacious sentry walks on the battlements and the chapel on the hilltop, the Prince's pride was deeply hurt, for it was apparent that he owed the capture of the Castle to neither his cunning nor his reputation as a feared warlord, but merely to the trifling fact that the besieged had run out of water – in view of the prevailing unusual drought, an unbearable condition for both man and beast.

The more Báthory found himself impressed by the peasants' castle, the greater his fury...

Soon after the siege by Prince Báthory the Castle's well, which later on became famous, was driven into the lime rock on which Rosenau Castle stood. It once ranked, together with the well in Belgrade Castle, as the longest in South-East Europe. However, at the beginning of the 17th century the 450 feet deep shaft of the well was driven into the naked rock and stone stratae by immeasurably hard work and primitive instruments. With gunpowder being finally introduced into war-craft and with improved firing techniques so ended the era of places fortified by towers and battlements.

Rosenau, situated at the crossroads of several Southern Carpathian passes and probably one of the most beautifully positioned market towns in Transylvania, both before and after being taken by Báthory's men, has been plundered, burnt down, destroyed and reconstructed dozens of times. In the 13th century, the Mongols on their way westwards and on their return on the roads of the Carpathian passes did not leave a single stone standing in this market town; that same century, and in the next, they came back over the passes several times, each time killing the very young and old and abducting women and men. Although nearly totally depopulated, the village managed to recover. With the cruelty characteristic of all Asian armies in the 15th century the Janissaries burnt down everything here which found itself facing their horses' hooves. Once more the inhabitants, who had taken refuge in the Castle, took to reconstructing the town. In the 16th century the troops of Walachian voivodes raiding the town cut the people up into pieces, stole everything in sight and set fire to whatever they fancied. Still, the town managed to recover. In the 17th century the troops of the Hungarian princes attacked and reduced the town to ashes. Once again the inhabitants reconstructed it.

Despite all these atrocities, despite the plague, cholera and earthquakes, the generations of peasants living here, starting in the 13th century, turned the Castle, high above the market town, into the largest fortified structure in the Carpathian Highlands...

This Castle and its well, together with one hundred and sixty of originally three hundred castles, fortified churches, keeps and town fortifications represent a stone monument of architectural brilliance unrivaled in this region since the Middle Ages. These medieval fortified structures have preserved the occidental face of the Highlands like no other architectural element. Nowhere else in Transylvania have historical events moulded the landscape more obviously than here in

'The Black Church of Kronstadt,' charcoal drawing by Fritz Kimm

44

Right: The Protestant parish church of Mühlbach

Below: Circular window in the ruins of the former Cistercian Abbey of Kerz

Following double page: Chapiters on the western portal of the Church of Reichesdorf

the valleys and plateaus above which the powerful strongholds, built of grey limestone and red basalt, rise high into the sky. In the south they dominate the still existing villages around Kronstadt on the Plateau of the Burzenland, which was settled by the Teutonic Order at the beginning of the 13th century. In order to find architectural structures of such awesome splendour one would have to travel as far as the South Tyrol, the Provence or the regions of the middle Rhine. Nowhere in Europe were so many castles and strongholds built in an area of the same size.

Most of them lie off the main roads. But anyone who undertakes to roam about the hilly plateau between the valleys of the rivers Alt and Mieresch, about the Terra Borza – the Burzenland – in the extreme southeast or the district south of the upper Samosch near Bistritz in the north, will see them behind each bend in the valley, from each boggy part of the terrain, from each mountain range barraging the cross-country roads.

They tower in the countryside like myths and legends.

Some of them were conquered, razed and reconstructed as often as ten times, in fact, the monumental Tartlau Castle near Kronstadt thirty one times, even more than Troia. There are others which no one, neither Mongol hordes nor Janissarian troops, was able to reduce. Others still, which had been burnt down and had slowly rotted away because their defenders, their women and children had all been slain and thrown to the vultures, served as quarries for neighbouring villagers, who used their square stones for the construction of their own houses just as their forefathers had incorporated stone blocks from the ancient Roman roads crossing the Highlands into the building of many of these castles.

As one roams around the country one can see them like some grey giants or like pale-red gnomes high above the roofs of the towns and villages. They are, all of them, weather-beaten, and a dull melancholy hangs over them but, more importantly, they are all marked by a relentless solemnity. For they are neither the product of merely fanciful pleasure in construction by some wealthy noblemen nor the result of true thirst for power and ostentation by brutal tyrants. They were built out of pure necessity. Their façades unflinchingly watched the oncoming waves of powerful peoples, whose one and only interest in life was killing for the sheer love of killing. Hence their solemnity is their pathos. Without exception they are, each and everyone of them, the expression of an unnerving submission to God's will – as if they cannot and will not avoid their fate. Where they rise in the sky as fortified churches, as places of worship with keeps and battlements, with projecting machiolations and archer slits above the side aisles, with wells in the central nave and choirs raised up to bastions, with double and threefold lines of walls encircling the peasant villages of the Highlands, they are the heroic and at the same time humble incarnation of this and other worldliness, something which consternates us because wise men tell us that it does not exist.

We know nothing about what the leaders of the legendary disciplined Mongol horsemen and Tatar divisions, Kuman and Turkish

Peel-tower of the church in Hetzeldorf

Right: The Protestant parish church of Mediasch

Below: Birthälm, the former seat of the 'Saxon bishop'

Horsemarket and Honterus Grammar School in Kronstadt

Horsemarket und Black Tower in Kronstadt

armies felt, thought or exclaimed at the sight of these fortified structures. They certainly roused their anger and fury to a very high degree.

Large-sized or even giant towns, such as Samarkand, Tashkent or Tabriz, Constantinople, Belgrade or Vienna, which were conquered, razed or, at the very least, besieged and whose inhabitants were massacred, offered an area of attack of an unusually strong potential of resistance but at the same time could be taken with one attack. Once overrun, they opened the gate to whole regions and countries.

The area here, however, was different.

The hundreds of fortresses scattered about the Highlands like hedgehogs, appearing at every step over the tousled manes of horses, these nests of six-foot thick and sometimes up to 45 feet high walls and strong towers springing up all over Transylvania like traps or snares, in particular after the Tatars' assault and the Turkish wars, must have given the Highlands the appearance of a confusion of bulky, interlinked obstacles. According to military historians the capture of these fortresses would have cost far too much time. The fact that the Ottoman armies – the military super power of the Middle Ages – bypassed the Carpathian Highlands when advancing on Vienna, after some of the best among them had gotten their heads broken at the passes, bears eloquent witness. Most important was that these fortified structures, erected around the towns and villages by the burghers and peasants, held back the Ottoman military forces which would otherwise have been used by the grand viziers in their march on Europe. One of the large-scale battles in these Highlands was fought in the 15th century at the northern approach to the Red Tower Pass – the Alt river was said to have been red for days from the blood of the Janissaries massacred to the last man.

There are no historical records detailing the route taken by the Franks, accompanied by Flemish people. These Germanic people, who in the middle of the 12th century started out from the districts of the middle and lower Rhine and came to the Carpathian Highlands, became the creators of this world of castles. On horseback, on foot, with women and children in wagons they crossed half of Europe, covering a distance of more than 1,500 miles – at first along the Rhine to Cologne, then eastwards to Magdeburg, at that time a prospering town famous for its economy, law and missionary work among the Slavs. From there they probably went southeast to Silesia, along roads taken before them by the Vandals and other East-Germanic tribes on the way south, crossing the historical region of Zips and pushing from the north into the inaccessible Highlands: into the green and boggy darkness of the Carpathian forests, whose clearings were inhabited by the descendants of ancient tribes, which had passed through this region during the migration of peoples, and were continually combed by shepherds and posses of Asian horsemen.

The leaders they followed must have been hard and bold men. Despite the dangers they were, above all, drawn by the spell of freedom. "Frank' means 'free, bold man'. Freedom had been and continued to be the leitmotif of their existence. One of the proudest verses of their early poetry says: 'To the Free I will travel . . .' 'For an honest

Preceding double page:
The village of Großau, view over the fortified structure

Right:
The village of Groß-Schenk, tombstone of Paul Whonner, 1639

58

59

man,' recorded one of their chroniclers, a bishop, as late as the beginning of the 20th century, 'freedom means more than the fatherland'. Strangely enough, later on they became known as the Transylvanian 'Saxons'.

It must certainly have been the dangerous instability of this region which persuaded the Hungarian royal house to take the momentous step of inviting these road-, town- and castle-building Franks as 'settlers' to this open province, which was safeguarded only by some abatis and flood-gates in the east and southeast.

Seldom, in history, have settlers been given a more trusting free hand. Indeed, around the middle of the 12th century, after a margrave of the Arpadian King Geysa II – Bán Belos – had negotiated with the Chancellor of the German Empire – Wibald von Strabo – the feasibility of settling these people, we find in the documents of the Royal Chancellery and in letters written by members of the Hungarian court, mentioning these people for the first time, the word *'hospites'* meaning 'guests'.

It remains an exceptional case in history that these few 'theutonici' and 'flandrenses', or whatever else contemporary chroniclers might have called them, did not die out soon afterwards in the wild carousel of these Highlands but, on the contrary, became their sculptors from the first moment of their arrival.

They not only survived physically – in hideouts and shelters – but with an unprecedented energy took to reshaping this region after the catastrophies of the migration era. They gave it what it had not possessed for seven hundred years: stability, moderation and character.

The villages and towns which they founded in the 12th and especially in the 13th century – Hermannstadt, Kronstadt, Klausenburg, Weißenburg, Mühlbach, Bistritz, Mediasch, Schäßburg, Sächsisch-Regen, Broos –, their ecclesiastical architecture with its crowning glory, the hall church in Kronstadt (later on called Black Church) – all this produced an urban look which brings to mind the medieval architecture of the Franconian district with its places like Nördlingen, Rothenburg ob der Tauber or Dinkelsbühel. Despite its ever increasing isolation they managed to incorporate this landscape into the same framework of occidental civilization which Tuscany, Gascony, Castile, North German brick architecture or Gotland claim for themselves. The phenomenal feature of this process lies in the fact that it took place in a region which geographically lay beyond the boundary fixed by Metternich – much later, of course – as being the outer fringe of Vienna: 'This', the Imperial Prince from the Rhine is said to have observed with a disdainful shudder, 'is where Asia begins...'

The explanation for the century-long prominence of this group of people, which in good times bordered on a quarter million souls, and the decisive influence it had on the peoples of the Southeast searching for their own identity can be found only in their disposition and the standard of values.

Stolzenburg peasant in his traditional Sunday coat

Covered market-place in Bistritz

Schäßburg Castle

63

Churchgoers in Deutsch-Weißkirch

In this connection we have the following picture:

Historians agree that among the Germanic tribes the Franks had the greatest talent for organisation and politics. They were not only the invigorating force in occidental history but through their sense of community they were also the driving force in the unification of the Germanic tribes, which had fallen out with one another. So it is no wonder that a splinter group of them, with the same disposition, founded one of the first republics in Europe, moreover in the South-east, which was free of feudalism. They founded a community which was the only one of its kind in Europe, in that on its territory, the 'royal soil', it did not allow serfdom or hereditary nobility.

Equally important is the standard of values they took with them as a guideline for their thinking and doing: and, during their trek to the Southeast, the middle of that century is in every respect a time of remarkable European proportions and dimensions. The Hohenstaufen Emperor Frederick Barbarossa began to determine the field of politics. The epoch-marking architectural styles of the Romanesque and Gothic periods encountered one another. It was the time of famous minnesingers, one of them was just starting to write the 'Nibelungenlied', while Wolfram von Eschenbach in his 'Parzival' would set the mighty Klingsor in Transylvania. The word 'German' appeared. At the same time Genghis Khan was born in the Mongolian steppe, and returning Crusaders – it was the zenith of the Crusades – brought back to Europe the plague, the Black Death. And it was also the time of Henry the Lion, who, in 1158, founded Munich, and the epoch of the great cultivation of land, namely that between the Gulf of Finland and the river Save – the so-called East-German Settlement –, which was carried out by German knights, monks, peasants, burghers, miners and merchants.

Those Westfranks and Flemish people whose creaking wagons were rolling from the Rhine via Magdeburg and Silesia to the Southeast played an integral part in this giant trek.

Without an understanding of their disposition and standard of values one cannot explain their beginnings in the Carpathian Highlands. It was the stubborn defense of their Western identity which enabled them to follow an independent development. Not even their grandchildren changed these ways; to have done so would have robbed their historical existence of all its meaning, it would have signified their end. It will signify their end if they do.

In the basic construction and shaping of their castles and fortified structures one can see how closely and at the same time loosely knit is their connection with occidental history. This is evident not so much in the urban fortifications, such as Hermannstadt with its thirty nine towers, built in the style of early medieval European towns and regarded as impregnable, or Kronstadt with its twenty eight powerful bastions, keeps and five fortified gateways completed under the personal supervision of the Emperor Sigismund, but rather in the fortifications erected by the actual peasants and numbering at one time as many as three hundred.

65

Right: The Protestant parish church of Bistritz

Below: View of Hermannstadt, colored copper engraving by L. Beyer, about 1840

These fortifications are to be found in an area stretching from the Baltic coast, via northern and southern France, to the Mezzogiorno; from the Rhine and the Nahe river as far as the wooded valleys of Thuringia from Württemberg to Styria and the Wachau as well as beyond the vast Pannonic Basin, on the Plateau in front of the Carpathians. Their network marks the boundaries of occidental Europe. To it belongs the wonderful world of the Transylvanian castles. The most noteworthy feature, probably, is the fact that during their entire history those who erected and defended these castles never themselves actually launched any act of military aggression . . .

It is the tendency towards the artistic which distinguishes the castles of these Highlands from others – both individually and as a whole. In no way does their shape upset the spirit and the law of form of the surrounding landscape from which they emerge. This consideration belongs not only to the realm of aesthetics, where empathic and creative powers have always been the essence of true art, but it is also one of the distinguishing features of all the significant works of architecture in Europe's cultural landscapes – Hellenic architecture embellishes perfectly the mountains and hills of Argolis, Phocis, Arcadia and Attica.

Only in this way can the tremendous variety of these stone monuments, their cracked and scarred faces dominating the Carpathian passes and river valleys, be explained. Although similar to one another in hundreds of ways, not one of them is an unimaginative copy of the other. Those who want to have a deeper understanding of them should make their way to them through the valleys and basins lying in front and absorb a part of this landscape before finally reaching them. Only those who approach them leisurely from a distance and from various directions, only those who absorb them bit by bit holding a dialogue with them as it were, will appreciate that their architects were acting like genuine artists when developing their towers and masonry directly out of a mountain range, rocks or hilltops, as if they were the natural continuation of them.

He who discovers this artistic feature will succumb to their fascination.

The Castle of Deutsch-Weißkirch in the northern foothills of the Geisterwald has a different architectural rhythm than the ruins of Stolzenburg Castle towering above the Basin of Hermannstadt – both of them were adapted to the spirit of the landscape in which they stand. The powerful accord of the walls with the towers encircling the Church of Birthälm differs from that of Michelsberg Castle, at the exit of the Silberbach-valley, not only because the former was built around the year 1500 A.D. and the latter around 1200 A.D. but because, styles and periods apart, its surrounding landscape radiates a different aura. Just as Rosenau Castle with its spacious composition cannot be fully appreciated without considering its stark mountainous background, so Törzburg Castle, built by the Germans of the Burzenland Plateau on the Dietrichstein, remains puzzling without taking into account its position at the entrance of the pass between the Bucegi massif and the Königstein Mountain.

Fortified church of Deutsch-Weißkirch

Hermannstadt: Approach to Town Hall through Pempflingergasse

The old Town Hall of Kronstadt

Despite their spiritually close relationship, no castle or fortified structure in the Carpathian arc can be replaced by any other. Therefore, all these varied and at the same time closely interrelated fortified churches, castles, keeps and gatetowers look as if they grew out of the ground as its natural children. Thus, for the people born in these Highlands they form an integral part of their lives.

Ruins of the ancient church of Urwegen

74

Transylvanian Verre Églomisé

Hermannstadt (Station Square Chapel):
head of Christ (16th century), part of a
monolith which used to stand in the
open field in front of the
Elisabethstattian Gate (today's Station
Square)

The Madonna is crying.

Tears, big as glass pearls, fill her dark eyes. Slowly, almost hesitantly, they roll down her iridiscent brown cheeks and onto the dark-red wrap draped around her narrow shoulders. Her head is inclined in pain and below it, in the far distance, hangs her son on the cross, unreally small and with his loins wrapped in a cloth of pale blue. The tears of his mother wet his naked, pain-racked body.

In the sky above black flowers, olive-green clouds, ochrecolored twigs of blackthorn as well as apostle heads, stars and ice-grey ribbons are gathered together in a circle of uncomprehending sorrow. But around the Madonna's head the glorious goldleaf of the halo shines radiantly. With the brightness of thousands of heavenly crowns it outshines all sorrow, making the tears sparkle until they reach the coarse fir-wood frame and disappear into its grain – like rain drops which seep away into dry soil and are lost forever.

The Mother of God is crying. The peasants stand in front of her, without comprehension, and cross themselves. They fill the small, dim church hall, fragrant with the smell of incense. They make way for those pressing forward, they kneel and look up at the one picture in the iconostasis from which, in the gleam of candlelight and oil lamps, an incessant stream of tears rolls down . . .

Verre églomisé (glass painting) of a religious nature is to be found scattered throughout Transylvania – in the soft light of Romanian farm-houses, in the Carpathian villages of the Alt Valley, in the Romanian wooden churches of the Marmarosch region which, with their Gothic-style decorations, are reminiscent of the European North, and in the churches of the Burzenland. Together with the crying Madonna of Necula, dating back to 1699 and year after year visited by thousands of peasants and shepherds, these icons are the expression of that Greek-orthodox devoutness which received its form in the very ancient European Southeast and which the rationalist and mentally shallow Europeans find so difficult to understand but today still shapes many classes of Romanian society. The spiritual experience that can be drawn from the Transylvanian icons resembles that to be gained from the monasteries and churches among the ruins of the Byzantine town of Mistras, in the Eurotas Valley near Sparta, or that in the soft golden light of the Ossios Lucas Monastery near Delphi.

Transylvanian glass painting, following the tradition of the famous icon painting of the Southeast, is, however, not only the latest movement of its kind in European art but at the same time perhaps the most profound expression of Romanian folk art altogether. Icon painting – the painting of the images of saints on wood, which goes back to the portraits on coffin lids of the first centuries after Christ – was practised very early on in Moldavia and Walachia, the two mother countries of Romania. Glass painting, however, was practised only in Transylvania.

The report on the weeping Madonna in the village of northern Transylvania was also the first anyone knew of this folk art; it was practised from about the middle of the 17th century until the beginning of the 20th century. In the eyes of the Romanian farmer it has always had something mysterious about it, as if it were not created by human hand.

The *subject matter* was the same as in early Christian times; themes which were taken over first by Byzantine painters and were then used and continued by the School of Athos even after the decline of Constantinople in 1453. Its *language of form* dates from the Coptic art, which had originated from Hellenistic-Roman (and even Syrian and Arab) heritage and was practised in the region between El-Minja and Kenna, on the river Nile, and flourished in Cairene enclaves. The *technique* was brought to Transylvania by travelling tradesmen from Austria, Bohemia and Bavaria during the early Baroque period.

Paintings of this kind contain elements of oriental carpet ornamentation as well as elements of Western European book decorations, which themselves, in fact, derive from oriental patterns. In an astonishingly creative process of recreation the Romanian peasant painters, however, achieved a remarkable independence of expression, which bears testimony not only to an ability to form their own spiritual environment but indicates also an unusual artistic talent. Transylvania, rich in the folk art and creative imagination of several peoples, has nothing else which could be compared with the sensitive world of colors of this glass painting – probably a result of the Romance part of these peoples' genealogy.

Schools teaching the craft of glass painting used to cover the Carpathian Highlands from their transformation into the woods of the Marmarosch, in the northeast, to the area around Kronstadt, in the southeast, from the settlements of Necula and Gherla, near Klausenburg, via the rural region of Mühlbach and Hermannstadt to Kerz, Arpasch and Fogarasch, situated on the banks of the Alt river. Though different in style, each of them produced master-pieces the beauty of which began to arouse interest and consideration only this last century. Craftsmanship which for several generations was passed on from father to son often developed into an art which prompted connoisseurs to award these peasant painters a place next to the luminaries of universal culture. It is naivety which is the chief characteristic of this art; one which derives its wisdom only from the inner reflection on things and for which striving for technical perfection seems to be unimportant, if not to say immature and undignified.

The kind of presentation used by Transylvanian glass painters bears out this fact quite clearly – their pictures disregard all the laws of perspective, anatomy and naturalistic coloring. It is also of some cultural-historical interest to know that the paper-thin, hand-made rippled glass, on which the masters of Necula, the Altland villages or the famous Şcheiu School in Kronstadt used to paint their saints in mirror writing technique, more than often came from the glassworks of the Transylvanian Germans. Likewise, the colorful mosaic windows of the Church of Saint Mary in Kronstadt (today known as the Black Church), which were destroyed by fire at the end of the 17th century, had come from a glazier's workshop in Rosenau as early as in the 14th and 15th centuries. So, too, did the painters from Arpasch, Kerz and

Gothic winged altar-piece in Tartlau

Fogarasch buy their glasspanes from a German glazier's workshop in the Alt plain.

Another remarkable characteristic of this mode of painting is the use of unchanged patterns for many generations, remarkable because this led to an unparalleled degree of perfection.

All of these Madonnas who have their heads inclined in the same way, all these Prophet Eliases driving skywards in multihorse carriages, all these Saint Marys praying, folding their hands and keeping their heads bowed at the same angle, all these St. Georges killing dragons or all these Josephs and Marys spreading their arms out over the cradle with the same gesture were conceived and treated differently for the two hundred and fifty years of Romanian glass painting by the various painter dynasties and schools. Very rarely, however, was a painting executed without that inner vibration which marks the beginning of each school of art and which, according to Goethe, makes up the best part of Mankind.

Again it might be of some cultural-historical interest to note that the patterns passed on unchanged for two and a half centuries from generation to generation were not only the result of some strict guidelines but also belonged to the curiosities born of fortuitous reality. For example, the hand taking an oath or making a blessing with the fourth finger – the ring finger – bent inwards, something which runs through all two millenia of Christian art and until today has been interpreted as having some inexplicable ecclesiastical significance, probably goes back to a pathological contraction of a tendon in the hand of John the Baptist: the so-called Dupuytren's contracture, as recent medical interpretations of icon painting have shown. This hand, a truthful copy of the ancient realistic sketch, has also been cropping up in all Transylvanian painted glass up to this century – Saint Haralambyos, depicted by masters from Kerz, raises his hand in this way, so does St. Nicholas and, on the glass panes of the painters from the region near Kronstadt and in the Marmarosch, the four Evangelists do it, Christ does it at the entry into Jerusalem, the Last Supper and at the Resurrection.

Time and again the individual pictures of this peasant art are of a moving beauty whose effect increases in accordance with its naivety. But it is only when they are gathered together as an iconostasis – on that railing dividing the public from the altar – that they exert all their force of splendour. At Easter Mass the flickering light of innumerable candles in the hands of the crowd of believers, some kneeling, others standing, makes the pictures of the iconostasis, hidden behind the glaze of the irregular glass panes, the triumphant manifestation of heavenly incandescene – that celestial glory proclaimed by this faith. The saints with their golden haloes stand near one another or above each other in solemn peacefulness and dignity: a passive yet still vivid picture of detachment from the earth and the world. There are Transylvanian iconostases in glass painting, for example, in Saint John's Church in Kronstadt, whose interior splendour shows the tremendous extent of Byzantine devoutness. Thus, the Romanian painters of these Highlands took on this Orthodox heritage of art, which had reached them in a roundabout way, as the last links in a chain of famous followers of this style and continued to cultivate it. With their iconostases painted on glass they recreated the last popular echo of the grand processions of saints which had reached their zenith in the Ravenna mosaics of the 6th century and can be seen in St. Apollinare in Classe or San Vitale.

Here, however, the peasant glass paintings are also a document of both the historical and the intimate life and existence of a people.

On the one hand they are the mute language of a people whose history was often artistically expressed in intense shows of mourning, for example, in the manifold variations of the Madonna benumbed in pain on the foreground of a black sky – a Madonna whose appearance and dress is always that of a Romanian peasant woman – or the 'bocet', the lamentation of the dead at the open coffin, where the cries can be heard resounding in the valleys of the Ore Mountains, in the Eastern and in the Southern Carpathians.

On the other hand the peasant painters tried, whenever possible, to portray in their pictures the every day and occupational forms of their people's life: Adam and Eve appear as a farmer's family working in the fields; the Archangels Michael and Gabriel wear peasant festive costumes with decorated highboots and leather waistcoats, and the landscapes seen in the background often show the silhouette of Romanian peasant villages in Transylvania.

From time to time shyly, as though filling the space between the all-mighty saints, motifs appear in some corner of the pictures, ones which point to the darkness of the historical threshold through which this people entered into the consciousness of others: the shepherd tending his sheep – a man with a head-high alpenstock, a fur hat and a fur cape reaching down to his ankles. The same outfit is worn today and has probably been worn by the shepherds in the Carpathians since prehistoric times . . .

Here ends the cycle of the patterns used in Transylvanian glass painting, here the great spiritual arc returns to the soil from which it rose – for Man it is 'earth to earth'.

Shepherds, Hunters, Farmers and Nomads

Transylvania, sweetest homeland!
Our forefathers' cherished home!
Now we greet thee in thy beauty
And 'round all they sons in duty
Cross the arms of harmony.

(Last verse of the Transylvanian-
Saxons' national song)

Shepherds at breakfast

Gipsy-hut near Baassen

The mother of 'Bulibasha'

Left: Romanian peasant from northern Transylvania

Below: German peasant attending service in the Church of Wurmloch

'Fair in Hermannstadt,' 1789. Water color painting by Franz Neuhauser the Younger

Just as the Swiss nation is made up of Germans, Italians, French and Rhaeto-Romans, so the inhabitants of the Highlands, at the foot of the Carpathians, are made up of peoples whose dispositions and mentalities are totally different. Conscious of their different descents and historical backgrounds, their different conceptions of themselves, they have, nevertheless, been living together in this landscape for about seven hundred and fifty years – next to each other, against and for each other.

First, there are the Romanians, the result of the encounters between Thracians, Slavs and Romanens; their history begins with the shepherd. Then there are the Hungarians or Magyars as they call themselves. They are members of the Eurasian-Finno-Ugric race and first made themselves known in Europe in the 9th century as hunters and warriors. Then, too, there are the Germans, whose existence is based on sedentary farming. Lastly, we have the gypsies or 'thingano', the Greek name for a sect in Asia Minor. They had been roaming about West Asia for hundreds of years before they were finally driven to South-Eastern Europe by the hordes of Timur Lenk in the 14th century.

The profiles of their characters are drawn, however, not only by the differences inherent in their archetypes: the shepherd, the hunter and warrior, the farmer and the nomad. Their characteristic features are marked additionally by four completely dissimilar languages of different origins, by four different denominational and religious minds, which add new dimensions to the genetic ones, by four almost hippocratically definable and totally different temperaments, which received their historical moulding in four geographical regions that lay wide apart from one another.

The differences in character between these four peoples are best manifested in their folk art, i. e. in a field where – in ignorance of foreign criteria – they follow exclusively the 'impulse of their hearts' when singing, dancing or writing poetry. Judging by West European standards, Transylvanian folk art is unbelievably rich and varied – it ranges from folk songs to peasant embroidery and weaving, from folk dances to early popular ballads, from wood-carving to the shaping, coloring and decorating of festive dresses with precious stones or metals, from customs based on the seasons of the year and dating from pre-Christian times, to pottery and goldsmithery. The charm of this varied folk art lies not only in its sharp contrasts, the differences in styles or its interpretation but also in the mixtures to be found at the intersecting points of their encounters.

Those who, for example, compare German peasant embroidery, which is well-balanced and infused with the characteristic sense of orderliness, with the folk embroidery of the Transylvanian Hungarians, will soon detect the essence of the different mentalities and characters.

The single-mindedness of thoughtful planning, which involves determinedly every single detail in the whole, transforms the needlework of the Germans into the picture of a long-term and structured pattern. No matter whether it be a mythical bird or stag, a rosette, a winged lion or foliage or the particular arrangement of these single parts into one composition, the sense of orderliness always seems to be the principle aim of the creation. It becomes clear that sedentary man is at work. His thinking is long-term, with thoughtful calmness he arranges all those things which because of existential considerations must be long-lived. Thus, the designs of this particular art of embroidery become the expression of a race of people who have the urge and the ability to create a community. It is no coincidence that these sweeping embroidery structures, kept mostly in soft red and blue, are dominated by an elaborate art of stylizing. The music of the delicate, sometimes strangely interwoven but still distinct ramifications can be compared to the polyphonic lines of the great composers. Their philosophical leanings are obvious, all the more so as their rhythmic patterns are the mental reflection of the world.

With the Hungarian counterpart things are totally different.

Here, the floods of decoration pour passionately onto the linen. They swarm out and spread proliferately into all directions with an impact that confuses because it seems to be wayward and uncontrollable. The colors are often of agressive and challenging brightness, the contrasts – fiery red and green on white ground – as well as the whorled patterns are of an inflammable liveliness that gives priority, at all costs, to emotion. In the panorama of these embroidered hieroglyphs motifs appear which go back to the great ancient steppe cultures, for example, the dragon or those animals with the lively, sweeping lines which can be seen on the two thousand year old saddle cloths from the Altai region. However, it is not only historical events but still more the pulse of a particular way of life which throws interesting light upon the Hungarian patterns. Is it not the horse-riding hunter and warrior galloping out into the landscape who, a millenium after he had become sedentary, is recognized immediately in the typical designs still used by the Hungarian embroideress?

In the same way the horseman is reflected in Hungarian folk dances – they are danced as though the dancer were sitting on the horse's back and the jolting body of the cantering animal was throwing him up into the air; his feet clash each other as if he were kicking the belly of the horse. The Hungarian national costume, too, with its tightfitting men's trousers, will always remind one of riding breeches.

The unruliness, the unrestrained exuberance of this former nation of horsemen becomes obvious, last but not least, in the magnificent wood-carvings on the gates of the farm houses of the Szeklers, living on the inner fringe of the southern East Carpathians. It looks as if the bubbling composition of grooves and cuts was fighting off restraint and trying to break through the edges of the trimmed treetrunk, as if still tempted by the expanse of all those landscapes that the Magyar horsemen used to roam about and conquered before they settled down in these Highlands and became Christians. In these woodcarvings, which echo incidentally certain ornamental elements of German origin, the relationship to a group of ancient civilisations finds its expression – the beginnings of the steppe culture of the Eurasian peoples in the heyday of which a great part was played by the Magyars,

Ancient wooden gate with carving in the Szeklers' country (southeast Transylvania)

Late Gothic door in a town house in Bistritz, 1480

the Scythians, Sarmatians and Huns, go back not only to the 8th century B.C. but also show connections with Far-East civilizations.

Anyone looking at these wood-carving visions will probably be touched by strange sensations as soon as the sunlight falls on them at an angle and they appear from the wood as ragged faces – they look as if the wood carver had for long periods of time not only been guided by a subconscious memory but also by a dark, melancholic longing for the merry independence of his primeval existence. Art, and all the more folk art, is not only the reflected image of its creator as the total of his being but also delves into the depths of his subconscious historical background.

It seems to be characteristic that the Transylvanian Romanian woman hesitated before taking over the embroidery patterns, which in the 17th century had come to the Carpathian Highlands in the form of the so-called Pattern Books for embroidery written by John Siembacher from Nürnberg. Before that, they had already been known in the Alpine region, in Venice and in other parts of Western Europe. While the German peasant woman regarded the close spiritual relationship with the patterns used in Western and Central European castles and nunneries until the end of the Middle Ages as an opportunity to continue the noble heritage, the Romanian woman kept to the geometrical designs already known by the Illirians and Macedonians. These patterns were used for both embroidery and weaving and as such had been known in all South-Eastern Europe – by people who had formerly been mostly pastoral. The patterns are arranged in stripes which can be prolonged infinitely: the ornamentation does not strive to be fitted into a static composition. This process, which can be used other than just in weaving, can be observed on every Romanian apron, pillowcase and hangings.

Are they not the artistic reflection of the shepherd's life, who, according to the calendrical rhythm of the seasons, wanders about the plains between the mountain ridges and river meadows?

All Romanian folk dances are pastoral dances – even the dancers' accessories, such as the little bells which they fix onto their feet, the peasants' shoes tied at the ankles with leather straps, the cries and shouts of joy are characteristic features of the shepherd. The dances of the archaic yet, in part, still existent pastoral cultures range from the *Sirtaki* of the Greek shepherds, both on the Island of Crete and in the Taygetos Mountains on the Peloponnese, to dances in the Croatian Karstland, the Montenegrin round-dances in the Dinaric Alps and the Romanian *Invîrtita* in the Southern Carpathians. In the eyes of the South-Eastern Europeans, the Central and West European dances with their predetermined movements are no more than colorless counterparts of their own dances, which are full of a spontaneous expression of joy and sorrow. They reflect the shepherd's way of life. For the same reasons which compel the farmer to follow an unshakable sense of orderliness, so his way of life and his conception of the world are bound to be different. This can be illustrated by the following example: While the structure of an early popular ballad of the Germans in these Highlands ('Der Rächer' – The Avenger) resembles that of a

Bronze font in the monastic church at Schäßburg Castle

98

Above: Service in Hetzeldorf

Right: Deutsch-Weißkirch. After Sunday service

fortress, so the most beautiful ballad in Romanian popular poetry, about the Carpathians, has the feel of a mountain river flowing down over the stones and fields of the shepherd's land – with no end and no restraint. In this ballad the same impression can be derived as in Romanian embroidery and weaving. The title of the ballad gives us a foretaste: '*Miorița*' is the Romanian pet name for a small sheep – an animal which more than any other makes the soul of the Romanian shepherd vibrate.

Just as this light-footed animal with his shepherd is always connected with the archetype Romanian, so the temporary structures which the shepherd erects during his short stays bear the characteristic traits – from the birch-rod fence in front of his hut, which nowhere in the Highlands strives for the massiveness of the German farm-house,

Above: A group of peasants from Deutsch-Weißkirch going to church

Left: Pastry cooking in the Szeklers' country (southeast Transylvania)

Dancing on St. Peter and Paul's Day in the village of Wurmloch

Left: Sunday in a Szeklers' village

to the mature art of icon painting, where the colors are put on the glass in an almost playful manner.

There is no lack of examples to illustrate these points.

Finally, there is the music of the Transylvanian gypsies expressing both joy and despairing sorrow. Furthermore, the almost crude pleasure in bejewelled decoration and attire is surely a clear sign of the origins and historical ways of a people who have always lived in uncertainty, somewhere between hope and despair and whose own rules advised them to pick up everything on the way in order to survive. The dozens of glittering necklaces around the necks of gypsy girls and women, the oriental garishness of their clothes, the unrestrained exuberance at any minor event – isn't all this the result of adapting to a bitter and hard way of life forced on them by powerful nations who formed the archetype of this group of people so much that it has remained obvious until today – as is the case of the archetypes of the rest of the Transylvanian peoples?

Who does not recognize today's picture of these Highland peoples in the features that have just been listed?

Even there in classical Transylvania where they encountered and overlapped each other they remained noninterchangable – for example, where the Romanian glass painter took over Central European patterns and adapted them to his own; where the German farmer of northern Transylvania absorbed into his costume of Flemish origin the Hungarian colors or geometrical designs of the Marmarosch Romanians; or where the Hungarian integrated into his folk music the gypsy musical scale based on c-d-es-fis-g-as-h-c. Only the fringes, however, of the four peoples' essential being were colored or influenced – the basic substance has, with an astonishing resilience, remained unchanged.

Beyond all differences, the peoples of these Highlands have always gotten on well with each other, as long as no foreign power disturbed the cycle of their own ways of life. History, however, always means that which takes place now, here, everywhere. It never ends. There is no escape, nor the possibility of refusal. The attempt to break out is the same as the attempt to ignore it.

It seems to apply all the more so in this region. To this day it is one of the most restless landscapes in Europe. The continual coming and going, appearance and disappearance of peoples blows through it like the breath of almighty time, determines the heartbeat of its epochs and seems to be its cardinal and inexorable law. Peoples and tribes lived here and died here, were crushed and wiped out by stronger ones, were absorbed into the stream of new arrivals or broke away to other regions – hurled out of the volcano funnel of these Highlands on the fringe of Europe . . .

Weekly market in western Transylvania

Gypsy girl

'Once upon a time there lived a fair maiden (in Stolzenburg) . . .'

Right: Peasants in their beautifully stitched Sunday coats in the village of Girlsau

Below: Transylvanian-Saxon women and girls in the Church of Wurmloch

Transylvanian-Saxon traditional costumes: Stolzenburg

... Wurmloch

Romanian winegrower's wife

Young woman from Girlsau with traditional head-dress

Front room of a Romanian farm-house from the village of Drăgus. Brukenthal-Museum, Hermannstadt

Front room of a Saxon farm-house. Brukenthal-Museum, Hermannstadt

'History – today, here, everywhere.
It never ends . . .'

116

Transylvanian towns and villages with their German, Hungarian and Romanian names

Abtsdorf a. d. Kokel – Ţapu – Csicsóholdvilág
Abtsdorf – Apoş – Apátfalva
Agnetheln – Agnita – Szentágota
Almen – Alma Vii – Szászalmás
Alzen – Alţina – Alcina
Arbegen – Agîrbiciu – Szászegerbegy
Arkeden – Archita – Erked
Attelsdorf, Billak – Domneşti – Bilak
Azuga – Azuga – Azuga
Baassen – Bazna – Felsöbajom
Baierdorf – Crainimăt – Királynémeti
Batiz – Batiz – Batiz
Batsch – Baciu – Kisbács
Bekokten – Bărcut – Báránykút
Bell – Buia – Bolya
Belleschdorf – Indiciu – Jövedics
Benzenz – (Binţinţi) Aurel Vlaicu – Bencenc
Billak – siehe Attelsdorf
Birk – Petelea – Petele
Birthälm – Biertan – Berethalom
Bistritz – Bistriţa – Beszterce
Blasendorf – Blaj – Balázsfalva
Blutroth – Berghin – Berve
Bodendorf – Buneşti – Szászbuda
Bogeschdorf – Băgaciu – Bogács
Bonnesdorf – Boian – Alsóbajom
Botsch – Batoş – Bátos
Braller – Bruiu – Brulya
Brenndorf – Bod – Botfalva
Broos – Orăştie – Szászváros
Bukarest – Bucureşti – Bukarest
Bulkesch – Bălcaciu – Bolkács
Burgberg – Vurpăr – Vurpód
Burghalle – Orheiu Bistriţei – Óvárhely
Bürgesch – Bîrghiş – Bürkös
Bußd b. Mühlbach – Boz – Buzd
Bußd b. Mediasch – Buzd – Buzd
Denndorf – Daia – Szászdálya
Deutsch Budak – Budacu de Jos – Szászbudák
Deutsch-Kreuz – Criţ – Szászkeresztúr
Deutsch-Pien – Pianu de Jos – Alsópián
Deutsch-Tekes – Ticuşu vechi – Szásztyukos
Deutsch-Weißkirch – Viscri – Szászfehéregyháza
Deutsch-Zepling – Dedrad – Dedrád
Diemrich – Deva – Déva
Dobring – Dobîrca – Doborka
Donnersmarkt – Mănărade – Monora
Draas – Drăuşeni – Homoróddaróc
Dunesdorf – Daneş – Dános
Durles – Dîrlos – Darlac
Dürrbach – Dipşa – Dipse
(Sächsisch-)Eibesdorf – Ighişu Nou – Szászivánfalva
Eisenmarkt – Hunedoara – Vajdahunyád
Elisabethstadt – Dumbrăveni – Erzsébetváros
Engenthal – Mighindoala – Ingodály
Feigendorf – Micăsasa – Mikeszásza
Felldorf – Filitelnic – Fületelke
Felmern – Felmer – Felmer
Felsendorf – (Felţa) Floreşti – Földszin
Fogarasch – Făgăraş – Fogaras
Frauendorf – (Frîua) Axente Sever – Asszonyfalva
Freck – Avrig – Felek
Galt – Ungra – Ugra
Gergeschdorf – Ungurei – Gergelyfája
Gierelsau – Bradu – Fenyöfalva
Gieresch – Cîmpia Turzii – Aranyosgyeres
Gießhübel – Gusu – Kisludas
Großalisch – Seleuş – Nagyszöllös
Großau – Cristian – Kereszténysziget
Groß-Eidau – (Iuda Mare) Viile Techii – Kolozsnagyida
Großkopisch – Copşa Mare – Nagykapus
Großlasseln – Laslea – Szászszentlászló
Großpold – Apoldu de Sus – Nagyapóld
Großprobstdorf – Tîrnava (Proştea Mare) – Nagyekemező
Groß-Schenk – (Şincą Mare) Cincu – Nagysink
Groß-Scheuern – Şura Mare – Nagycsür

Groß-Schogen – Şieu (Mare) – Nagysajó
Großwardein – Oradea – Nagyvárad
Gürteln – Gherdeal – Gerdály
Hadad – Hodod – Hadad
Hahnbach – Hamba – Kakasfalva
Halvelagen – Hoghilac – Holdvilág
Hamlesch – Amnaş – Omlás
Hammersdorf – Guşteriţa – Szenterzsébet
Hamruden – Homorod – Homoród
Haschagen – Haşag – Hasság
Heidendorf – (Beşineu) Viişoara – Besenyő
Heldsdorf – Hălchiu – Höltövény
Heltau – Cisnădie – Nagydisznód
Henndorf – (Hendorf) Brădeni – Hégen
Hermannstadt – Sibiu – Nagyszeben
Hetzeldorf – Aţel – Ecel
Hohndorf (Hundorf) – Viişoara – Hundorf
Hohe Rinne – Păltiniş
Holzmengen – Hosman – Holcmány
Honigberg – Hărman – Szászhermány
Hundertbücheln – (Hundrubechiu) Movile – Szászhalom
Irmesch – Ormeniş – Szászörményes
Jaad – (Jad) Livezile – Jád
Jakobsdorf b. Agnetheln – Iacobeni – Jakabfalva
Jakobsdorf b. Bistritz – Sâniacob – Szászszentjakab
Jakobsdorf b. Mediasch – Giacăş – Gyákos
Johannisdorf – Sîntioana – Szászszentivány
Kallesdorf – Arcalia – Árokalja
Karlsburg (Weißenburg) – Alba Julia – Gyulafehérvár (Károlyfehérvár)
Kastenholz – Caşolţ – Hermány
Katzendorf – Caţa – Kaca
Keisd – Saschiz – Szászkézd
Kelling – Cîlnic – Kelnek
Kerz – Cîrţa – Kerc
Kirchberg – Chirpăr – Kürpöd
Kirtsch – Curciu – Körös
Klausenburg – Cluj-Napoca – Kolozsvár
Klein-Alisch – Seleuş – Kisszöllös
Klein-Bistritz – Dorolea – Asszubeszterce
Klein-Blasendorf – Blăjel – Balázstelke
Klein-Ilva – Ilva Mică – Kisilva
Klein-Kopisch – Copşa Mică – Kiskapus
Klein-Lasseln – Laslău Mic – Kisszentlászló
Klein-Probstdorf – (Proştea Mică) Târnăvioara – Kisekemező
Klein-Schelken – Şeica Mică – Kisselyk
Klein-Schenk – Cincşor – Kissink
Klein-Scheuern – Şura Mică – Kiscsür
Klosdorf – Cloaşterf – Miklóstelke
Kokelburg – Cetatea de Baltă – Küküllővár
Krebsbach – Crizbav – Krizba
Kreisch – Criş – Keresd
Kronstadt – (Oraşul Stalin) Braşov – Brassó
Kyrieleis – Chiraleş – Kerlés
Langenthal – Valea Lungă – Hosszuaszó
Leblang – Lovnic – Lemnek
Lechnitz – Lechinţa – Szászlekence
Lesch – Leşu – Les
Leschkirch – Nocrich – Újegyház
Ludwigsdorf – Logig – Szászludvég
Magarei – Pelişor – Magaré
Maldorf – Domald – Domáld
Malmkrog – Mălîncrav – Almakerék
Maniersch – Măgheruş – Küküllőmagyarós
Mardisch – Moardăş – Mardos
Marienburg b. Kronstadt – Feldioara – Földvár
Marienburg b. Schäßbg. – Hetiur – Hétur
Marktschelken – Şeica Mare – Nagyselyk
Marpod – Marpod – Márpod
Martinsberg – Şomărtin – Mártonhegy
Martinsdorf – Metiş – Szászmártonfalva
Martinskirch – Tîrnăveni (Diciosînmărtin) – Dicsöszentmárton
Mediasch – Mediaş – Medgyes
Meeburg – Beia – Homorodbéne
Mergeln – Merghindeal – Morgonda
Meschen – Mojna – Muzsna
Meschendorf – (Moşna) Meşendorf – Mese

118

The total production of this book was carried out by the Tyrolia Printery, Innsbruck, the layout was done by Walter Myss, the index of place-names on pp. 118/119 was supplied by Dr. Ernst Wagner.

Photographic credits: out of the 85 photographs reproduced in this book 49 were taken by Erhard Daniel, Regensburg. The rest of the plates were reproduced by the courtesy of the following photographers and archives: Hans Baumhartner – p. 13; Hermann Buresch – front cover and pp. 21, 26, 39, 53, 63, 83, 105; Josef Fischer – pp. 14, 17 and 34; Balduin Herter – p. 78; Karl Lehmann – pp. 30/31; Annemarie Schiel – rear cover and pp. 1, 25, 36, 54; German Foreign Institute, Stuttgart – pp. 94 and 100; Romanian Tourist Office – p. 112; Transylvanian Archives of Art, Horneck Castle, Gundelsheim on the Neckar (Rolf Schuller) – pp. 66 and 90/91.

Grateful acknowledgement is made to Heinrich Schunn for permission to reproduce the oil-canvas on pp. 18/19 and to Mrs. Dorothea Kimm for making available the original copies by Fritz Kimm on pp. 29, 33 and 45.

The map Transylvania/Sibenburgen reproduced on the front flyleaves must be credited to G. and J. Blaeu, Amsterdam; the map reproduced on the rear flyleaves to the author.

Translation into English by Anna Maria Kienpointner and Anna Nowicka.

Copyright © by Wort & Welt Publications Limited, Innsbruck · ISBN 3-85373-071-X

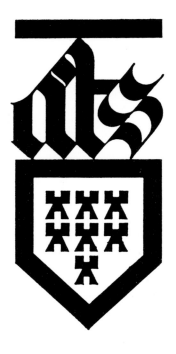

. . . the Transylvanian Saxons in America.

Immigration of the Saxons to America began in the 1880's, with the majority settling at first in Ohio and Pennsylvania. To fight homesickness, they gathered together to comfort and to help each other learn the language and customs of the new world. Soon small informal groups were organized to provide fellowship and mutual aid.

In 1902, the idea of bonding these local groups together as branches of one national organization, resulted in the founding of the 'Central Verband Der Siebenburger Sachsen.' In 1965 the name was changed to the 'Alliance of Transylvanian Saxons.' From a humble beginning of four branches and 252 members, the Society has grown to represent 34 branches and 9,000 members spread out in twenty cities and seven states. With an estimated 100 thousand Saxons and descendents in America, there is ample opportunity for much future growth of the society.

The Saxons in America, through the fraternal society have developed a wide variety of activities. They include a life insurance program; provision of benefits for orphans of it's members; publication of the Volksblatt, a weekly newspaper; sponsorship of cultural activities and events; support for affiliate groups such as the Siebenburger Sachsen Saengerbund, the Transylvanian Saxon Bowling League, and others such as local choral, band, cultural, and youth groups.

The Alliance owns it's Home Office building in Cleveland, Ohio, which provides an inspirational base for the fraternal operations of the society. A beautiful Cultural Room provides a colorful atmosphere for the display of art, handicraft, historical documents, and literature which portray the Saxon heritage and culture.

Today, as always, the Alliance is dedicated to an ongoing recognition and preservation of the customs and ideals that have made the Transylvanian Saxons a great people, proud of their heritage, outstanding citizens in the communities in which they live.

The Alliance is pleased to publish the English translation of this beautiful pictorial history of Transylvania and sincerely thanks the author Hans Bergel and the printing firm, Wort und Welt, for their cooperation.

Alliance of Transylvanian Saxons
Home Office · 5393 Pearl Road · Cleveland, Ohio 44129